ARE YOU GOING TO IMPROVE AS A WRITER OR JUST FADE INTO OBSCURITY?

An aggressive guide to the craft of writing, storytelling, and engaging readers.

BRANDON SCOTT

*For the professional writers
and the prolific storytellers.
You inspire me more than you can ever know.
Keep giving stories to mankind.*

Copyright © 2020 by Brandon Scott

All rights reserved.

No part of this publication may be reproduced in any form or by any means whatsoever without the prior written permission of the author except in the case of brief quotations embodied in critical articles or reviews.

Contents

Prelude 1: 1
The point of this book and why it's a little different 1
Prelude 2: 3
The obligatory instructions on how this book works 3
Beginnings of Books 5
What the Audience Needs to Know 8
Why Should We Care About This? 17
The Usual Options 20
Why This Person Is in This Story 24
Early Imagery 26
Dreams in Fiction 29
The Narrative Bite 32
Assignment 1: 34
Pushing the Rock Down the Hill 42
Burn It All Away 44
The Guide into a New World 46
Choices Need to Be Made 48
Assignment 2: 50
Growth or Shrinking 53
The Villain and Their Various Breeds 55

Power Over	62
Some Characters on The Side, Please	65
Reflections and Echoes and Similar	69
The Biggest Rule of Writing Characters	71
Assignment 3:	74
The Woe of the Middle	79
Repetition and Memory	85
Consequences	87
A Quick Note About Plot Twists	89
Assignment 4:	91
The Goal of an Ending	94
Justified Victories and Earning It	96
About Happy Endings	99
The Great Falsehood, Trick, and Misdirection of Fiction	103
Tying Up the Shoes of a Plot	106
Assignment 5:	108
Assignment 6 and Beyond:	111
Acknowledgments	117
About the Author	120

Prelude 1:
THE POINT OF THIS BOOK AND WHY IT'S A LITTLE DIFFERENT

Hello, hi, and howdy. My name is Brandon Scott, and if you are reading this, then you are here for some help in regards to stories. You want some assistance with the more technical side of storytelling or would like another resource in your cap for how to write books well.

You are also likely coming across this book because you've read the other two books in this series. Maybe you got your first book done with *Are You Actually Going to Write A Book Or Just Talk About It?* but felt like you still had a lot of room to grow as an artist? Maybe you even put out your first series thanks to *Are You Actually Going To Be Prolific Or Just Make Excuses?* and still didn't feel like you had a grip on what you are doing?

I can only speculate. But, if that's anything close to the issue, that is *why* I am putting out this third book. Because there are gaps in those other ones. I focused them on the actual process and the discipline of writing. I didn't get into anything deep on the topics of stories, of characters, of structure.

I didn't yet teach techniques and lessons on how to write books *well*.

This is partly because the best writing teacher is simply the practice that comes with writing a lot of words and reading a lot of other people's books. But, I am a qualified person to teach, and it will not hurt to improve at your craft and learn tricks you may not know.

But that does make this book different. The previous ones were very structured, with lessons and tasks I assigned to get people to the finish line.

This book can't be quite like that. I *will* give it structure; I will give assignments. I intend to guide you, dear reader, to the end of the book. But know this: there is no real end to its purpose.

This is a book on how to improve, rise, practice, and learn. But there is no mastering storytelling. It is simply not done.

What I can promise you is this: it is very possible to markedly improve. You can soar to new heights of skill, sometimes in a very short period of time.

But understand this too, I cannot give you imagination. I cannot give you depth, only show you how you might evoke it. Storytelling is a muscle that needs its exercise, and I can only show you how you might strengthen it.

So let's get started. There's a lot of ground to cover.

Prelude 2:
THE OBLIGATORY INSTRUCTIONS ON HOW THIS BOOK WORKS

I'd like to think that if you are reading this book, then you are familiar with how I structure these things. But, for those of you reading this as your first book in the series, I have a few specific rules about how you use my instructional books.

This is because I am very deliberate and specific with what order I tell things in and how and where I present ideas. I create these books to be lessons for the reader.

So, with that understanding, I hope it does not come as a shock I have a few rules.

They are not that complicated. The first is to not skip around. Don't jump from page to page or chapter to chapter. Read it all in the order I set them out for you. I will instruct where to read, how much to read, and where to stop.

I may also use terms or concepts you have never heard before. If that does happen, then I need you to go online or find a dictionary and discover what the word or term means. If you don't understand the meaning of what I am saying, then how is this book going to benefit you?

Finally, the assignments. This book is structured so you read some standalone or related references and then are given an assignment that should utilize what I just explained or taught.

I need you to do these assignments and not read past them until you do. I know what people are like, and they won't go back and do the assignments if I let them breeze through the book.

So, it's not allowed. You do them before you read a single page more.

Okay? Okay. Now, read on until you hit the first assignment.

BEGINNINGS OF BOOKS

Because it makes the most sense to me, and I hope you, I will set out this book into three major sections with subsections of sorts. No points to you if you can guess those three sections.

This is because the three parts of a book are distinct in how they are done, in what is expected of them, and the challenges of doing each well. The hardest section is the middle, and the easiest is the beginning, but we shall get to all of that as we go along.

To begin, pun intended, we are going to first define what the needed aspects of the beginning of a story are. Then, we'll go into the sections and nuances of what I am talking about. If you've read any other books in this series, then I should warn you these sections may have assignments *within* them. You'll do an assignment for beginning a story and then read more about that same topic, and then another assignment on book beginnings.

But again, we'll get there when we get there.

Let's talk about beginnings, shall we?

The reason that beginnings are so easy for writers to think of and write is that beginnings are what hold all the exciting bits. The freshest tastes of world-building happen in the first few chapters. The characters get to show off their character traits in condensed form, and the gimmicks and premise of the story are shown off.

The beginning is a little like the author getting to invite someone in to see their new television or computer rig. All excitement and need for someone else to validate that it's worth the time and effort to have.

And that's all well and good, but what is the point of the beginning, structurally? Well, it does a lot of heavy-hitting—but it must do one thing above all: it must invite the reader to be part of the story.

This is multifaceted and continuous.

Assume nothing initially. The reader has never been here before. You need to get them rapidly familiar with the rules, the people, the location, the time, the tone of the story, the intents of the story, and so many more facets. You have to do it on every single page, and then pull the rug out from under them enough they are no longer comfortable.

Get them to accept this story house for what it is, then light the corner of the rug on fire and douse gasoline everywhere else.

If you did a good enough job, the reader will instinctually not want the flame to burn. The whole rest of a story can be carried on the back of that feeling. For other tales, the plot may require the characters find a new place to stay, or put out the fire, or learn that they can survive with the flames.

The rest of the story, somehow or another, addresses that fire. And yes, you can make an entire book about a literal fire.

You have to do this with grace and thought and planning, and most of all: *intent*.

Sounds difficult? Eh, it can be. Let's dig deeper into it.

WHAT THE AUDIENCE NEEDS TO KNOW

"Info dumping" is overloading the reader with information about the world, about the people, about background information or history, in a way that's jarring or confusing or boring. It is hard to parse or care about. This only gets worse the less your book is based on the real world.

Like, you can just say a story takes place in New York, and many people will get what that place is like by the simple fact of being alive. If your story is instead in the center of a planet that does not exist, then you will need to explain things, yes, but not all at once.

I will say this clearly: do not have a massive paragraph that explains something about the world. If you must info dump, you can have a single sentence or two that gives background world information.

Your reader needs to be gently led into a world, not slammed into it with a hammer of words.

So, how do you do this properly?

Well, here are the most important notes on world establishment, which I consider a precursor to world building:

1. What's normal is normal

2. What's weird is very weird
3. What implies more is implying a lot
4. The miscellaneous is the soul of a world
5. Give just enough for the next step

I will explain each of these in their sections.

What's Normal Is Normal

You walk down the street, and there is a small fiery demon that offers you condoms, and you do not react…except wave a happy hello. That either means you're insane, without emotion, or in this world that's just a thing that's been happening for a long time and no one (or at least not you) would find weird.

Humans eat the prepared flesh of animals from tiny plastic bags (beef jerky) and our planet drops the same substance that our body is mostly comprised of from the sky, regularly (rain). This, to someone from another dimension, might be a tad weird and odd.

But you usually don't even think half a second about it, yeah?

So, then, that's how you organically build a world from the first part of the story. What is normal is normal and is treated as normal. No one stops to explain that it is normal, because to people of this world it's just how it is.

This is powerful for storytelling and grabbing your audience's attention. As is the inverse.

What's Weird is Very Weird

If our condom demon is, instead, something that is not a part of the world, then we need to treat it with that mindset from the first moments it appears. Your characters have to react strongly to what is weird because the audience has no other metric. If they are only mildly surprised in their reactions, then your audience has to assume it's not common or regular, but not abnormal or fantastical.

Don't be comical with these reactions (unless your book is funny) but do establish there is something wrong.

I know it's very cliché, but there is a reason that "I'm dreaming, this can't be real" is such a common reaction to these moments. We all know that dreams are usually very strange affairs. If something in your world causes that reaction in a character, then it's a great gauge of weirdness.

Even if you have no character in the scene to react, you can still inspire that reaction in the audience by emphasizing the normalcy present in addition to the strangeness. A real city, a real location, on earth, in the year the book was written…then a condom-selling goblin emerges from the shadows.

It's weird, it's very weird, and we are all on the same page about that fact.

What Implies More Is Implying A Lot

Everything in your story implies something. Every choice means *something*—and you can and have to use that to your advantage.

If in your world everyone has a cell phone, that means that the infrastructure for a cell phone is in place so everyone can call each other. That means the location's technology is at a certain level, and that the society is at a certain stage.

It also means that information can move past an immediate location quickly, and that it likely will in the case of some insane event. If an explosion takes out a building, you can bet the survivors are calling someone about it.

And that's all from such a simple decision as what people have in their pockets.

You can and should be using this for more powerful things, like making the reader assume something about your world without directly saying it. This works in tandem with the "what's normal is normal" rule. If you have someone, as an example, not show concern when hit with a fireball, that tells you something.

That tells you a lot, either about the character, the world, or the magic that made the fireball.

This need not be limited to fantasy or science fiction, either. If you have a character react to another character drinking alcohol with surprise and maybe even disappointment that tells you a hell of a lot of information.

This can be done without being intrusive or annoying.

It also does something important for the reader. It gives them something to think about and wonder about and assume.

If you can get someone to wonder something about your story, then you have them by the nose, and can get them to read more of the book. Don't be vague to try to get this reaction—that's not the same.

You make them wonder why something is because they understand the circumstances enough to infer information.

Why doesn't she drink? What did she do that would make someone look so disdainfully that she did?

What is up with that fireball?

You must answer these questions—but not right away. Your readers have to turn some pages to get there.

The Miscellaneous is The Soul of a World

Okay, let's go over why I chose to have a condom-selling goblin as my example so often. I had a specific point to it.

It's that it is *ultra-specific*.

The specifics and the details are what make a world real. It's what makes the reader believe this is a real place.

You *can* just have a story with generic men sitting in generic chairs talking about generic cars but then *no one will care*.

You can also go too far the other way with this. You've probably read books that give you way too many details.

Used wisely, though, it's what makes a book stick in the mind. The right description can force an image into the reader, as if recalling a memory.

Vocabulary can aid this a great deal. The English language (I only speak English, but I assume this of other languages) has words that describe only one specific thing. With the right word, it leaves little room for anything else.

A calico-patterned tuning fork the size of a regular fork.

A camo-patterned woman's cardigan with a wine stain on the left sleeve.

A chrome fan that spins just a little too fast to make out the individual blades.

Did you see my pictures? Is it readily there as soon as you parse my words? If not, then I did something wrong, or you don't know the meaning of a word I used.

When you need to highlight something or give an impression of something, then go for the strange or ultra-specific details.

This is used in conjunction with everything else. Is the specific detail normal or weird? Does it imply something specific?

If you use these methods and use them carefully, you won't need to outright explain almost anything.

However, if you do still really need to explain something…

Give Just Enough for The Next Step

Sometimes, your audience needs to know something, and there is no easy way to tell them except to just explain it.

In that case, just tell them.

If there's absolutely no organic way to put in that pertinent data, then you just tell them. If all your characters know something, and have no reason to say it aloud, tell your audience the details.

But be sparing. When you do have to lay down an info dump, you give them just enough information they can understand what is happening. You give them enough that they can understand and maybe guess what happens next.

And that's it.

Stop right there.

And do it sneakily. You don't want to spoil something by being too obvious. But you also want the audience to know enough to understand what does happen.

If magic has consequences, and that is a big part of your inciting incident, then make that clear and communicated beforehand. Imply it if you can, but state it if you can't.

It is always better to have a story that makes sense and is emotionally true than to have a story that surprises. If you can't be subtle enough, and you worry they will get it too early, well, it's only the beginning of the story—it's okay.

You can surprise them later.

Just give what information you need to give.

—

Using these methods, all at once, can easily get your audience to buy into the story. It can get them to understand what is happening in a way that feels like exploring, like discovering, like being led on an adventure, instead of being taught.

It's more fun this way, and it will make your audience care much more about the story and its world and its characters.

It's not always easy—but when was good storytelling ever that?

Info dumps are the lazy way. They are not as effective, and they do little for the reader most of the time. They are much more potent when they are small and in the middle of books, just to fill in the slight gaps that maybe weren't implied heavily enough.

All other uses are usually just cop-outs.

So, paint your story dream in small pieces, and with the shadows cast by your gestures, and the way you say the words you do say.

WHY SHOULD WE CARE ABOUT THIS?

Your audience has no reason to care about your characters until you make a distinct reason for them to do so.

Just because they are the focus of a story, does not give us a reason to consider them anything more than a person passing us in a car. Even less so because we know they are not actual people.

This is one thing that, strangely, biographies have over a lot of other book types. We know that they are real and important people, so we buy in right away and care. The premise makes us care. We bought the book for this person's history.

As to other books, though, there's nothing intrinsic, and you have to yank the reader in.

But how do you do this? Well, there are quite a few ways.

Let's take, for example, caring about a character because we see something human in them we understand. If we, ourselves, are dealing with an emotional issue then we will buy into the character the moment we see them match it, because we instantly understand a part of them.

This is by far the most effective technique. Target the reader's human empathy and lean on relatable experiences, and you will get a rise out of someone.

But, if that option doesn't fit what you are trying to do, then there are a few others that are of lesser but not useless effectiveness.

One way is simply spectacle. If the first thing you see of a character is them performing something impressive, then that's an establishment of a character. You often see this in superhero or fantasy stories. A character's first action in a story can be to showcase the world's magic or demonstrate some talent.

Humans naturally appreciate shows of immense skill. Capitalize on that. But make it something that really does require skill and practice. No one cares much for naturally gifted characters who win without effort.

You can also purposely withhold information. Tease the reader with something fascinating about the character. If you have them do something unique or jarring while being careful not to explain too much why or how, then you have a mystery. I don't mean the genre; I mean a question the audience wants answered. I don't know much about westerns as a genre, but the stranger rolling into town that no one knows is a trope for a reason.

You can also try to up the likability of your characters. You might consider making them funny, or wise, or extremely kindhearted. You could make them easy to cheer for. Underdog characters are common for a reason.

Characters are best when they are based on universal emotions, then trickled down into the specificity of individuality. They need not be deep or extremely developed: so long as they are not boring or bland or generic, you're on to something.

You can overdo making your characters resonate. But under-doing it is far more dangerous.

Ask yourself why someone should care about your characters, and find a real answer, and then work from there.

THE USUAL OPTIONS

I want to make something very clear. I do not think that a book starting these ways is necessarily a bad thing. Some strong books start with these intros, and they work well with them. A story must be judged by its ability to entertain, inform, or allow the reader to escape from all that ails them.

However, I want you to know that these intros are done so often that they can have a stigma attached to them. You must have a reason for using them, instead of simply wanting to do so. Some readers will actively and immediately disregard you if you use these intros.

I'll list them in no particular order:

- Starting off dead or dying.
- Starting off in a dream
- Morning routine

Starting off dead or dying

Death is something intrinsic to life and is terrifying—so it makes for quick and effective attention-grabs. But it's also been done so often that it is little more than expected now.

Starting with a character dying, coming back to life, or injured to where they are about to die is, yes, an opening guaranteed to grab someone's attention. It's interesting enough they might read on to discover what is happening...

...but you've also killed your momentum by front-loading it.

If someone dies right off the bat, then they are already dead once, and we do not fear for their life as much in dangerous situations. You have to do something different than violence to make the audience care now.

Of the openings being discussed, I chose this first because it's the least cliché. It still works well if you can back up the drama of death with whatever comes next. If you are doing a story about the afterlife or immortals or bringing back people from the dead, then it's just a natural place to begin. It's fine as it is the whole concept of the story.

Just don't overdo it, and don't expect people to be on board with the opener every time. Like I said, it's common—and common is not surprising.

Starting off in a dream

I will talk a *lot* more about how you can use dreams in a story, and where it is okay to do so. But I will also say now that you should not use this option almost ever.

It's a false start, a cheat. You are not starting your story here. You're starting and stopping a story only kind of connected to the one you are working on later. You are also sacrificing a moment to establish your main character with real context.

Again, I will cover more about what dreams are good for in storytelling, but don't use them in your beginnings unless it is very important to do so.

If it's just that you can't think of an organic way to cram in some cool visual or foreshadowing, then you have problems bigger than me banning you from writing a dream sequence.

Just pick some other way to introduce your story. Something that concerns what is going to happen, really, *in* your story.

<u>Morning routine</u>

Tell me if you've heard this one before:

A girl, usually teenaged, wakes up and looks around her room. We learn about her just from how the room is set up.

She goes to the bathroom and looks in the mirror. Then, as if she has never seen her face before, describes her hair color, eye color, and maybe how she feels about the way she looks. She'll usually dislike something or think she looks too plain.

She then may describe what her plan is for the day, then go into the living room/kitchen where her parents and siblings are. Cue those characters being introduced, and the opening parts of the plot discussed over breakfast.

You have seen this scene before. It is one of the most cliché tricks there is. Even stories without this specific structure will start a story with the main character waking up.

There's a lot of reasons this exact scenario is so ubiquitous: you get a lot of information across quickly. The main character's physical description is handled, even when you're writing in first-person and would not usually have an excuse for that. You have a sense of their life, location, and a lot of telling hints about them as a person.

It seems so economical. And it is. Shame everyone *ever* does this. Shame it has been used so often that people will hold it against the story if you do this, with no further context or chances to impress.

So, if you can, you should not use this intro. Try something else, anything else. You do need to spell out your main character's physical characteristics. You do need to set up plot details and plot trajectory. You do need to have a way to introduce characters—but you have to be more creative than doing what everyone else does.

There may be no new stories, but there can be new ways to introduce them. And I suggest you think of them.

WHY THIS PERSON IS IN THIS STORY

There's comedy potential in placing the wrong character in the wrong story. A badass in a lighthearted romance can make for some funny moments. However, if this is not your story's gimmick, you need to ask yourself this question about how you will proceed: Why is this person going to have this happen to *them*?

If the story is disjointed from the main character, then it won't matter much what happens. If a confident character is in a story that focuses on fear, then it may not achieve cohesion—unless their stoicism is part of the point.

A character must match their plot. If you are talking about life in suburbia, but your story is about a person who lives in a city—then it's likely to fall a little flat.

A character whose whole thing is a struggle with a crippling fear of ducks should not be put in a story that focuses on an invasion of alien slugs. That just doesn't sit well and does not have a structure, a point, or an end goal.

There are so many ways around this rule, but you need to think about *who they are*. You need to know why this story is about *them*, specifically. You can put in too much of a cliché just as easily as you can end up with someone in the wrong story. The cliché is better in this case if you must choose.

Make a character or a plot idea, then make someone or some event that matches the other. Then you will find cohesion.

EARLY IMAGERY

Within a few pages, there are a few relevant bits of data you need to establish. They can be dropped with the weight of a cinderblock or gracefully inserted like an assassin's blade between the ribs.

They need to be said, somehow, or your audience will simply assume something semi-random. If they are not told these things they may even become confused, disoriented, or think you are trying to trick them. A severely enough uninformed audience will assume you are misleading them or hiding information for a twist.

If you do not mean to mislead, then be sure to include:

Some Physical Features:

You can never control exactly how your audience sees your main character but be sure to leave information they can think with as they read. I recommend, at the very least, saying hair and eye color and age and some indication of skin tone and body type. That will give a general idea of what they look like, enough for someone to put in their own imagery.

Past that, you should at least include some distinct feature—if relevant. Off-color hair, scars, injuries, robotic parts, alien features, a signature glove, etc. Whatever it is, also mention it when you can.

Their Name:

Even if your main character is just named John, you still should find an excuse in the story to tell the audience that. You would introduce yourself to a stranger with your name, yeah? So, make sure your reader has been given that information. You can even do it by having the main character introduce himself to someone, or directly to the audience.

Just make sure they know their name.

It's not even just for the story; it will also make your job easier. Try juggling pronouns if three characters all use "she/her." If you don't give them names, you'll have to use sentences like "the one who just waved said 'Hello'" or some other clunky method.

If you don't want your character to have a real name, then use a nickname or some "The Noun" template. It just needs to be something that you can call them, and that your audience can use as a reference point.

Location and Era:

You can imply this stuff if you don't want to reveal it. You also need not be specific. You can have your story just kind of be "in New York" or "some magical castle in the 18th century." That's enough.

Giving a location grounds the reader. It gives the story an essence; it gives expectations. It does a lot to establish tone and genre and even story pacing.

It can be a subtle touch, but don't neglect it. Even if in your story it doesn't matter where it takes place, someone will still care enough to wonder. You may as well give them that.

The only time it can backfire is if you don't know that location well. If you have never been somewhere, then research it, or don't use that place. People will notice.

I'm from Florida. If you tell me a character is in Orlando, in the summer, and has had little water, I will wonder why they didn't get heatstroke.

Don't do that. Just give us a place for the story to exist.

-

None of this should be hard or challenging for you to include as the writer. Each can be done in a sentence or two, so long as you put in the thought.

Just find a spot for them. They really help.

DREAMS IN FICTION

Dreams in fiction should only be used in four ways. The main three are prophetic, symbolic, or informative. The fourth option is having a story take place entirely or partially in a dream world. In those cases, you need to make it very clear as soon as possible that it is a dream world.

For all other instances, there are the three.

A prophetic dream is common in fantasy or science fiction. It can result from a superpower or a chemical that allows someone to see the future. The point of these dreams is to show what will happen or has a possibility of happening. This option is often stronger if the main character acknowledges and knows of its prophetic nature—if not at first, then after a few times.

The second is the symbolic dream. These can take a lot of forms and often depend on the reason for the dream. They are dreams that represent something about the characters, like their emotions or fears or desires, but showing them in a way that's loose and illogical.

The trick here is to not be too obtuse with them—unless the dreams are upsetting and horrific. Characters tripping hard on a drug is a common way to do this for horror, as is a spell or curse that shows a character's worst fears.

This one is the easiest to mess up and yet the most powerful in terms of visual storytelling. It allows symbolic communication of character's innermost thoughts. Use them wisely. Use them to mean more than they show.

The third one is only allowed in a few ways. It's useful in a world where dreams can be a form of communication. Between a character and a god, or a connection between two people bonded by something supernatural are acceptable applications. You cannot use this if you have not set it up, unless this is you setting it up.

The point of these dreams is to say or show something that the audience or the characters could not know without someone telling them about it.

There's often an inclination for this to be a good way to set up backstory. You can start a story with a character dreaming about the major traumatic moment in their past that informs their personality. You can show it in real-time instead of telling the audience about it later.

Now, all three of these may sound well and good and might serve you well in your storytelling avenues—but they also do something bad. Depending on when you use them, they will weaken your story considerably.

The issue is that *all* stories are dreams and you are letting your reader into one anytime you are writing. Thus, and especially if the dream sequence is long, you are setting up rules and worlds and thoughts and implications, and then removing them and starting over from scratch.

The reader has no way of knowing, except savviness, that this is not the way the rest of the book will be. If you make them comfortable and then rip it all away with it being a dream, then you have to start over with establishing the book. The reader has no idea what's still in the rules. In the waking world, they don't know what carries over to the next part of the story.

I'm not saying that dreams have no place in fiction. They can be used to great effect, even if they are at the beginning of the story. But understand that they are a very risky proposition. Dreams should be baked deeply into the story, and both be *heavily* acknowledged as dreams and—if somehow magical—be explained in the world as a thing that can happen.

You may think dreams aren't supposed to have consistent rules. They don't in real life. In fiction, they absolutely have to have some semblance of reason or logic or purpose or you are just showing off. Your audience is not here to see what weird things you can come up with. Your audience wants a story.

THE NARRATIVE BITE

For some of you, this may be useless advice. You may not even need to worry about this. But, for those of us on the edgier side: remember that audiences can become desensitized to almost anything.

If you intend to shock your reader, there are rules. If you put something more horrible than anything else that happens in the book at the very start, then you've wasted your chance.

How could you hope to shock them now? You've already used your best trick. You've used the strongest blow you can manage—all else now is just flailing.

Your audience, if you intend to make a work particularly gory, extreme, or upsetting, should be aware early of that fact. Give them that so they can know if the story is for them. Let them decide if they are mentally prepared for that kind of story. Give them a taste, but you shouldn't use the biggest blow to begin.

You build to that. Context makes for impact. A character we've never met before being reduced to chunks matters little compared to when it happens to someone we've grown to know.

Violence, gross-out, and shock have diminishing returns in storytelling. You only get to use them so often—and, if you do them without levity between, they wear out even faster.

I am not judging those who think their story needs something fucked up. I've written much of that myself. But, if you are going to do something messy, then you best do it artfully, and with control of the impact you are causing.

Assignment 1:

Whereas most of my books are full of very definite instructions with endpoints, this book is about writing training. So, as to that intent, there will be instructions you can do and finish—but they will be more like practice.

You can do them as often as you feel like you need to until you get the point of the step.

Now, a note. A big note. These instructions and orders will be hard, frustrating, complicated, and annoying. The tasks I am asking you to do might seem stifling or arbitrary. I have reasons. These steps will knock you out of your comfort zone, teach you why stories often are the way they are, and hopefully help you grow.

Also, do each of these at least once.

1. Pick a genre you would like to practice more in and become better at writing. It need not be the genre you usually would write, though it is not a bad idea to also practice in that space. You can always get better at writing something. You can always improve. If you want to do this with multiple genres, then go ahead—just repeat the steps for each.

2. After reading the following instructions, write an opening scene/chapter. No more than 1500 words. I have *many* rules about how you will write it. You do not have to follow these when you write an actual book. Most books start how they do for a reason—and the things I ban here are tried-and-true ways to engage readers. Please do not feel like I am disapproving of using these things in real books. Some of my favorite books/movies/shows/video games have these tropes. However, to train and learn, these are your constraints:

   a. Your first paragraph cannot contain or allude to or happen directly afterward or even suggest anything to do with the following:

      i. Violence, injuries, scars, or blood.

      ii. Anyone being chased, hunted, pursued, or watched by someone or something unknown or known.

      iii. Death, dying, resurrection, the afterlife, Heaven, or Hell.

      iv. Monsters, demons, zombies, or any other supernatural creature.

      v. Superpowers of any type.

    vi. Obviously magical items (especially swords), magical people, or mysterious phenomena.

   vii. Any made-up-by-you proper nouns.

  viii. Dreams or hallucinations or prophecies.

    ix. Waking up, either from regular sleep, passing out, or because of something mysterious.

     x. Amnesia or the inability to recall recent events.

    xi. Rain, snow, strong wind, storms, hurricanes, or other severe weather phenomena.

b. On the other hand, your first paragraph or page must manage to do the following things I'm about to list. For extra training, you'll want to do this in a way where it is not immediately obvious that is what you are doing.

      i. Show your main character doing something that establishes a strong and distinct personality trait. It does not necessarily have to be a positive one.

 ii. Find a way to state your main character's name.

 iii. Get across your main character's basic physical traits.

 iv. Give a clue to where the story is taking place, regarding time and date and year, geographical location, and, if relevant, planet.

 v. Establish something that your character is failing at or would need to improve on to succeed at something.

 vi. Make the reader empathize, on a visceral, universal level with your main character.

c. By the end of the section you are writing, you will need to make sure that you have done the following:

 i. Had two or more characters talk and interact meaningfully, not just small talk. It also cannot just be insults or just using their conversation as an excuse to state some plot-related information. You can have dialog like that in the section—it just can't be the *only* dialog.

ii. Unless you are writing a story where this would not make sense (like a world of all clones or a completely alien-populated world), you must include a character or characters who are a different age or religion or gender or sexuality or race or ethnicity, etc. as the main character. The world has many varied types of people. Reflect that. If you do not know how to write any kind of person not exactly like you, then you need to get out more. It's not a perfect substitute, but you can also go online and find information on the culture or history or experiences of people and read first-hand accounts. Do not assume you understand them just because you've seen people "like that" on television or have heard/seen a few stereotypes. Do your research.

iii. Hint at, but do not outright state, a prevailing theme for your story. Something core that the story wishes to tackle. This can be a very simple theme, but there must be a theme, and you need to bring initial wisps of it at the offset.

iv. Create levity without having a joke. Something with unbridled humanity at its center. It can be literally anything, and it can still be tinged with sadness. A single star in the night sky through a broken rooftop, perhaps. You need to establish an essence of hope, of humanity, of joy, or of laughter in this first scene, no matter how dire the story is intended. You are a writer, and you must be able to manipulate your reader's emotions in both directions.

3. Now, after writing all of that to the best of your abilities—no matter how difficult it might be to do so—you are going to compare. There are

two steps to this, and they are both important. It doesn't matter what order you do them in. Just do both within about 48 hours.

    a. Get a copy of a recently popular book. Something that nearly everyone's read or at least heard of. Something that got made into a movie or a television show. Now, read the first chapter. I do not mean a prolog or narration or flashback or little opening section; I mean the first real chapter. Spot the point where you cared about what was happening in the story. Look for the instant, the sentence, that got you to empathize with the main character.

    b. Now, while still following and doing every other rule, write an opening section. Write it with as many things I banned in Step 2, Part A as possible. As much magic, death, dreams, storms, chase scenes, and violence as you can cram in there. Go nuts with it. While you do, pay attention to everything you are doing. Notice how fast you are writing, how easy or hard it is to come up with an idea, how the writing makes you feel. There's much to learn here.

And that's your first assignment. It's a doozy, I know, but this step does a lot of things for you. It should expand your creativity, your options, and your tool kit. Storytelling is much richer when you can include new things and know why we use old things.

But, even with all that, we have even more to learn about beginnings. The beginning is quite a bit of a story. We have to cover its second half: the part where the beginning is broken, shattered, and becomes the middle of the story.

So, read the next section of articles, then get on to the next practice step.

PUSHING THE ROCK DOWN THE HILL

Okay, so, once you've set up the world and its rules and its characters, you must do more than just make them dance around for your amusement. You need a story that goes somewhere and does something.

It's a story, not a sightseeing tour of some world or location you created.

So, what kicks off a tale and makes it a tale?

The answer: whatever is normal, whatever usually happens, good or bad, *has to change*.

That's the only criteria. A winning lottery ticket, malfunctioning machine, solar event, nuclear war, a discovery of a love of knitting, or a crush forming. Anything that can change the trajectory of a person's path in life.

How dramatic you want to be is more a matter of genre and personal taste. The only thing to consider is your audience. What is interesting enough of a change for them to care?

If you've read my other book *Are You Actually Going To Be Prolific Or Just Make Excuses?: A Very Aggressive Guide To Fast Writing, Publishing, And Being A Professional Writer* then you'll know this can be part of your story "gimmick." Suitably unique or jarring happenings can be enough to interest your reader.

This is why violence or death is one of the most common of the story starting options.

But, again, it doesn't matter, so long as it's interesting. If a man finds out that his boss is secretly a collector of potatoes and has been storing them in the ceiling, and now he has to help him keep it a secret or he loses his job—that's going to get someone to pay attention.

Make them pay attention. That's always your job.

Do it as soon as you can.

BURN IT ALL AWAY

Wanting things to go back to how they were before is a common human reaction. Your main character, once they have something happen to them that is suitably dramatic and upsetting, will naturally want things to go back to how they were.

You cannot allow this to happen. There must be a reason this cannot be allowed to happen, and it needs to make sense.

If your reader wants to know why they wouldn't just turn right away at the first sight of an alien with two heads, then you have a problem. You must place down why the main character has to deal with the problem, or why they have no way to get out of the problem.

The most common way you see this done in a story is that the main character's parents are murdered, or maybe even their entire hometown is wiped off the map. This is a neat and tidy way to do this because you can't go back to a place that no longer exists. It's also a way to make your reader both emphasize with your main character and sets a personal reason for the main character to go out to defeat a villain.

Another common trick is they are being pursued by something or someone. They can't stay in one place for too long. Or they are special, magical, or dangerous, thus they might be discovered if they remain in one location.

You can also get a very definite version of this where the location they leave is inherently impossible to get back to without serious effort. If you teleport to the other side of the universe, and then the teleporter breaks, well…you get the point.

There's no right answer to how to do this. All that matters is it should somehow make the main character unable to return to how things were.

However, before you go off and think these all *have* to be negative: they need not be. I just focused on it because it's more common. However, simple knowledge of a treasure is enough to be a barrier back to normalcy. Knowledge, curiosity, or drive for a goal are all valid other ways to make it so your character can't go back.

Just make sure they can't go back.

THE GUIDE INTO A NEW WORLD

You may have seen this happen in a story before. You have a hero, usually a dorky white guy, who has just stumbled upon something that is beyond his old world, either literally or emotionally. He's scared, or in danger, or simply confused—and then a girl shows up.

A girl who is (by American pop-culture standards) attractive, powerful, and knows much about what is going on, and may even be directly related to the dangerous thing. She saves or otherwise pulls our main character out of the dangerous situation. Then, for the rest of the story, she acts as a source of explanation and defense.

So, yeah, this is a fairly common trope. It's common for a lot of reasons—some reasons unsavory or at least pandering—but there's a nugget here that's useful as a writer.

The idea of a guide into the new world.

When your character finds themselves robbed of the normal, a new character who understands the weird can act as a great way to get your audience back up to speed.

Now, it may suit your story better to throw your character(s)—and the audience—into chaos for quite a while, unsure of what the rules or situation is. You may not give them someone who can explain for some time. You may dial up the madness for sustained drama. But, if you intend to keep the story going, then you bring in someone who knows what is happening and can guide them along.

The guide may not even understand the full scope of what is happening. That's allowed. But they are almost always smart or wise or calm in a way that the main character is not, and thus can serve as an overseeing or helpful figure within the story.

However, they don't have to be good people, or on the side of the main character. To stretch the rules here, you can get someone who is still an explainer but is doing it for evil reasons. Villain speeches, for instance, still explain some fundamental part of the new normal and contextualize what is happening and will happen.

You can even have all this be done by an in-story book the main character reads.

If you find you need to constantly explain something that your main character could not know but would need to know for the plot: consider adding in a guide, mentor, or teacher character.

They serve a lot of purposes and make things a lot easier to organically be explained within the story.

CHOICES NEED TO BE MADE

A character must decide something in the story. They must make decisions, good or bad, that cause something to happen in the story.

This is very old and basic writing advice, but your main character needs to decide to do things at some point. The plot can happen to them for a little while, and they simply try to survive, but they eventually need to decide to do something.

Now, if you are wondering *why* this rule is true, well, it's because of how it affects the audience, not so much how it affects the events of the plot. You can have the plot just kind of do its thing and pull along your main character—but that's not something that readers enjoy.

It's more engaging, as, assuming we have connected to the character, we would like to see them make the right choices and have it work out for them. We want to root for their successes. Seeing someone, even fictional, make hard choices and then deal with the consequences and overcome those consequences can help the reader feel less worried about the same happening to them.

You could, in theory, make a story where a ball or something experiences the world around it and does nothing. We may, for a bit, become empathetic to the ball, but try to make an entire book from that perspective.

Choices move longer stories. Hard choices make interesting stories. You must make a character make them. Tough, awful choices. Strong, bold choices. Wrong ones that are deadly or dire mistakes.

Choices make for strong stories. The more the better.

Assignment 2:

I'm about to make you do some writing that may feel inorganic, and off, and rushed, and awkward.

That's okay. This is meant for your improvement, it's not for other people to see, or for you to publish. It's just weightlifting. Mental, yes, but still strengthening.

I want you to do the following repeatedly until you can comfortably think with this method. Do these steps, all the way through, at least twice. Past that, I leave it up to you to decide when you've gotten to where you can write the ending parts of a story's beginning.

1. List things that will change someone's life forever. Good or bad. Come up with at least twenty. And, yes, if you are doing this step for the second time, you need to make an entirely new list. They can be as mundane or as dramatic as you please. They can be as specific or as broad as you want. Just be sure that no matter what happens after them, there is no way to undo them.
2. For each thing on your list that's negative in some way, put next to it something someone might try to reverse it. Now, come up with why that would not work.
3. For the good outcomes, we are going to do something similar. Come up with something

that would *inhibit* the character. As an example, say your character just discovered that they have the map to a treasure, hidden for centuries, and it will be buried by a rockslide in the next week. However, they also have a job as a retail worker, and need to go in tomorrow for their shift. They obviously will quit and go for the treasure—but that is a choice that will change something. They have no source of income and may use up all their savings on this trip. That's what I mean. Come up with something like that for each good outcome.
4. Pick one of the good outcomes most interesting to you, and type out the specific scene—no more, no less—of a character having their world changed forever. It should be no more than 500 words. You need not have the moments before, the setup, or anything else to the scene. Just the moment it all changes forever. These are often enjoyable to write, as they are frequently dramatic and engaging and weird, so have fun with it.
5. Do the same thing as the step above, but with a negative one. Ham it up as you write it. Make it melodramatic. This isn't part of a real book anyway, so you may as well be as bombastic as you please. The point is to see how these scenes flow for you, and how they differ from each other.

Now, we get to go to the next section of a book. The biggest part of a book. The middle. We're going to do this in two parts. The first part will be about how to handle your characters, and how to deal with the growth of your heroes and villains and anyone else you use in your stories. The second part will be more structural. General stuff about how to get through the middle of a book.

It's going to be a little disjointed because the middle is specific to the story, and the storyteller. I am still including it, though, to give you tools to get through the murkiness that is the middle.

It's going to be fun.

Read on until you get to the next assignment.

GROWTH OR SHRINKING

The point of most stories is the journey of a character. We want to see how this adventure takes a character down a path and changes them. And most books on this subject will probably stress that the character needs to become more than they were before.

This is not true.

A story must have a changing character, but they can change up or down. A story—though it may be depressing—can be the undoing of a character. It can be the slow and gradual ruining of a person. The intense melting of what they once were.

A story can be about the falling moral code or the deteriorating state of the character.

These are typically called a tragedy.

So when deciding the passage of a character, and how they will become different during a story, remember, and remember well, that you must know where the character is going, but you don't have to make a story where someone gets better throughout.

False paths one way, then taking them down the other is always an option. Just make sure that the choices they make are the direct cause of the way they go. If they are going to fall, let it be because of something they did. A bad decision that caused them to gradually become less. They could have made it for good or bad reasons.

If they are going to rise, then make sure it is by their hard work. By their moral code. By their intention to do something good.

People like stories where characters earn what happens to them, one way or the other. Though it may make them sad, some audiences also like seeing the tragedy that can be the wrong moves, in the wrong order.

THE VILLAIN AND THEIR VARIOUS BREEDS

Not all stories even have villains. Some are more environmental, some are more personal, some simply are not a story with that kind of conflict. But, for when you do want to have someone evil, someone aggressive, someone as an opposition, there are many ways to take them, and they are often informed more by your main character than anything else.

If your villain is the main character, then the reverse is true.

To show you how to create them, work with them, I will go into the basic structure of villain types. There's almost a sliding scale of how to do them, and most villains can be tracked by this scale.

- Justified to Selfish
- Moralistic to Immoral
- Personal to Monolithic
- Comedic to Dour

I'm not going to draw that all out in some grid, but the point is most characters that are villainous are some degree of these. Let's go over each one, and I hope it will help you decide how you want to play with your villain. I'll present you with the most extreme definition of each far side of the scale. I leave it to you to work out the middle grounds, and examples in media you may have seen.

Justified Villains

A justified villain is somewhat or entirely right (at least in their head) for what they are doing, but still evil. They are doing something horrible, but the reasoning for it is logical to them.

Robot villains of this type commonly want to wipe out humanity because "human beings are too harmful to themselves." Fantasy ones may have been given some vision of the future and found it to be necessary to avert it with extreme force.

Selfish Villains

They are doing what they want to do because they feel like it, or want to, or simply have no reason why they *cannot* do it. These villains are often more powerful than most people, were never raised to have empathy, and can kill or destroy or manipulate with little effort. If they are not physically powerful, manipulation will usually then be how they achieve things.

They are also often motivated by simple stuff like power, gold, wealth, status, or something akin to that. They are simple villains to write and are not ones to make big speeches or something. You can have characters who are this but are trying to act like they are not—and the revealing of their nature will often be a pivotal scene.

Moralistic Villains

Different from simply having a reason for what they do that they feel is logical, these villains have a rule set. They do not kill, for instance, or they only do what they feel is necessary by the rules of some dark god, or something like that.

These characters' strict rules bind them.

You don't see extreme versions of these often, except with evil priests. They are rather one-note but can be done well in fantasy settings.

Immoral Villains

Psychopaths and rapists and mindless villains. These are simple, scary, and gruesome. They don't care; they do not have empathy and will simply kill or destroy without some underlying reason.

These are often more deranged than Selfish Villains because they are not even motivated by something as concrete as gold. They are more embodiments of evil than real people.

Personal Villains

Personal villains are personal to the main character, or at least a major character. They are someone's dad or mom or sibling. They are an old friend or a colleague or even a former ally to the hero. They know more about the main character than our main character would like or have more leverage over them in some other way.

This is often played as a twist or a later stage revelation, but it's also become somewhat cliché. A personal villain is a tool for drama, but it is not always a necessary drama. The big benefit is if the main character is unwilling to kill (or otherwise deal with) the villain because of the connection, and thus might have to grapple with that choice's consequences.

Monolithic Villains

These villains have nothing to do with the hero except being actively responsible for the bad things happening. These are often kings, gods, rulers of other types, or just people of some power and influence that are also evil.

These villains become increasingly dangerous the more aware they are of the hero.

The issue with these villains is they can be villainous in a way that is cliché, cartoonish in a not-fun way, or simply bland. Ruler villains who are just powerful or in a position of power and not overly smart or manipulative are more often guilty of blandness. Controlling a population by fear—without showing distinctly how this is done—is an old and worn concept.

Still, to have a story where the main character is not menaced by anyone directly for a little while (learning their powers is a popular thing to do during this free time), the lord or king or government official villain is a decent choice.

Comedic Villains

This is often a very likable villain. Villains with a lot of charisma, or a fun personality, or simply a bombastic persona.

Basically, how much do you want your audience to like your villain and enjoy it when they are around?

Just be warned, and warned well, if you do this too much then you might make it so your audience will be unhappy if they die or lose. This is especially true if you didn't make your hero likable enough.

Still, if you want a villain that sticks with people, and maybe even makes your audience want to see them in a sequel, this is a great option.

__Dour Villains__

These villains are not fun. They are hate-able or simply evoke little of a reaction from the audience except concern. They are cold, or ruthless, or unemotional, or mostly unseen. An enemy sniper might count as this. You can still explore their humanity and give them a personality, but the more you bring that out the less of a Dour Villain they are.

Dourness is best used for villains you want to be scary and genuinely provoke unease. The further you take them down this path, the less human your readers will perceive them as.

-

All villains, to some degree, are on these grids. You can choose to make your villain in many ways within it, and there are no bad combinations. Some are better suited for certain genres though, and some have tones intrinsic to them.

For instance, you would not want to put a Comedic Villain in a story that's meant to be very dark. Similarly, your child-friendly adventure story should probably not feature an Immoral Dour Villain, Personal or otherwise.

Villains are often a lot of fun to write, but there is a danger to it. If you're not giving them enough thought outside of what they do plot-wise, it can bite you. So, just understand the underlying mindset of a villain before you drop them into a story.

POWER OVER

When it comes to giving characters powers, there is a difficulty in not making that power too much. In making it so a character can handle everything thrown at them for the sake of making your protagonist "cool" or "awesome."

Look, giving readers a feeling of not being powerless is great, but making it ruin good stories is another matter.

This is why a lot of characters are not well-equipped to use their powers at first. They are either limited by skill or knowledge, and thus cannot blast their way through the villains of the story with ease.

And that's one of the best ways to do it. It makes for great power potential but then tempers it into a story with cool stages and plenty of dramatic moments.

But another aspect of the plot must be managed, and it may be something you've never thought of too deeply when you're reading a story.

And that's how the power of the hero compares to the power of the villain(s).

Overpowered villains are allowed and encouraged.

If your villain could easily obliterate the hero if taken on directly, at least at the beginning of the story, that's good stakes and a great way to elongate the story.

Thusly, there are two ways to handle the plot once this happens.

The villain either needs to be gradually weakened, or the hero needs to outclass him eventually. Which one you choose is better determined by if you plan on writing sequels or not.

The logic of this is simple: If your villain gets weaker, and then the hero beats them, then the hero's power and the entire power-level scale of the whole plot remains consistent. The villain was special, and thus can be removed, and thus we bring in a status quo. This way, when you write the sequel with your villain presumably dead and a new one rising, you don't have to write around your hero being godlike. You also don't have to de-power your hero by some shenanigans to get the plot back to having stakes.

The alternative to this is to make the next villain(s) a lot more powerful than the first one—since your hero is now a lot more jacked. There's nothing wrong with this approach, mind you, but you'd be amazed at how often you eventually have to make the villain a literal deity or godlike being. If you're not writing a plot where you can go that high, you may not have that much room to scale.

This is also a reason powers bound by very fixed rules are useful. Instead of taking the power higher, on either side of the conflict, you just get more creative with what the powers can be used for, and how destructive they can be. You go sideways with the potential.

If you've seen a show or read a book where at some point the rules had to be broken to make a fight fair, or eventually their powers devolve into who can blast out the biggest beam of energy, then you've seen what impact not planning for scale can cause.

Plan ahead with powers. Figure out their bigger forms, and how you want to escalate them, or you'll end up with boring characters and boring fights.

SOME CHARACTERS ON THE SIDE, PLEASE

It's an odd but prevalent temptation to stick a character in a place where they are alone, and then to just have them internally monolog.

I implore you not to do this.

It's boring, and navel-gazing, and, if allowed to continue for too long, it can make someone hate your main character.

Instead, make sure to—even if it takes a chapter to get to it—give them someone else to talk to and interact with within the plot. Even if it's just a kindly bus driver, you have to make your characters have some human contact.

People left alone will talk to themselves. Forced isolation can cause people to go insane. People need other people—we like to be around others and need company and companionship.

Yes, you can have stories specifically about a character who is shy or otherwise unable to form connections. But even those characters almost always end up with some crutch that fills the gap or one person they *can* stand.

Talking generally, you need to have characters come in for pertinent conflict and layered interactions and to form drama and such other narrative wonders. Thusly, you have side characters. And I think of them in two ways: persistent and ephemeral side characters.

A short explanation: an ephemeral side character only exists for a scene or two, and persistent ones are a core aspect of the story. The difference between a random schoolteacher for an exposition scene and a best friend character.

Let's go over ephemeral first, shall we? They aren't as important and thus can be played with on a different wavelength. We can also break them down into specifics even further.

Because you have characters that are part of the set. These characters can have little said about them. If your story is set in a school, then random students and teachers have to be there or it would be weird. They need not be described much.

Then you have characters with names and at least features to them. For these characters, though they may never come back, I recommend giving them surface-level aspects that can be summarized in a sentence. There's a fine line here of making sure not to draw too much attention to the character and making the audience think they matter more than they do. But mentioning that one teacher always had a faint smell of lemons and no one ever knew why makes the world feel more real.

Because we do have impressions of people that are one memorable trait. I'm sure you have someone you maybe saw on a plane or at a restaurant with some very notable aspect to them that stuck with you.

Add that in sometimes. It makes the world feel more real.

Then, finally, we get to persistent characters. Characters that do exist for more than one scene and have a name and a life or at least do stuff in the plot that suggests they have reasons for what they do.

There may be a temptation to over-design characters like these. To give them rich inner lives. You don't need to, though. They are only as important as they are for the story. Though stereotypes are not ideal in fiction, you can put in somewhat shallower fictional people when you need uncomplicated characters in your plot.

Take the generic bully character. They exist in fiction to this day for a reason: they are an antagonistic force that can either play a part in kick-starting a plot or simply serve as catharsis when they get beaten up.

You can also have crush characters that need not be much more than someone the main character likes— that they admire from afar. Sometimes, that's enough for a character. When dealing with these generics, I recommend figuring out what they look like, and what their general personality is, and basic data about their life. Do they have both their parents? Are they wealthy? Do they have any hobbies, especially abnormal hobbies? This is plenty for minor characters like these.

Then, finally, we can get to the side characters that are fully part of the plot. These are best friends, love interests, allies, etc.

With these, they should be treated as the main characters in terms of thought put into them. They can be thought of as having equal worth and vast inner and outer lives. You can map them out as thoroughly as you would the trajectory of the main character, and you probably should do so.

However, with one caveat. And it is a big one. You need not give them a big arc. You *can*, sure. The secondary characters—especially in a longer running series—should have arcs, both narrative and personal. However, in a standalone book, if you only give a single character significant emotional development, make sure it is your main character.

The world of a story needs people, and it needs some to be of lesser focus than the main character. Stories that focus on many, many characters can work—but they then must be fairly shallow, and you'll likely end up with a few core characters that grow out of that and become more, anyway.

REFLECTIONS AND ECHOES AND SIMILAR

Well it may not make sense for all stories, there is a tried-and-true way to make sure that your hero and your villain fit, and their conflict feels like it is important or potent. It's been done a thousand times and will work a thousand times more.

Your villain is a dark reflection of the hero. Simple as that.

But how to do this? Well, to make a villain that works with a hero, you must first understand your hero. What do they want? What are their methods and motivations?

What is their most critical flaw?

And it is here, or adjacent to it, that the reflection villain exists. They are the flaw but more deadly and dark.

Their goals are adjacent to the hero's goals. A villain may share the same goal but deal with it evilly.

The villain may be simply an evil version of our character, or a version of him that would exist if choices went differently.

Let me take you down a quick example.

Let's say your main character is a superhero that is obsessed with making sure a specific town is free of crime. He is a good person who does good things and spends all his time working on this specific goal.

So, what might his villain look like? Well, there are a lot of ways to go about it. One that make sense is a crooked version of him that kills the criminals he would normally arrest.

And our villain's definition of crime is a lot more…broad…than our superhero's. He kills people who litter, for instance.

Well, there's a dark reflection villain. He has, essentially, the same motives as the main character, but goes about it in a way that's horrible and twisted.

Your hero may even notice this and be distressed by it. Even if the hero doesn't, your audience will, and that will give them a new way to engage with the story.

THE BIGGEST RULE OF WRITING CHARACTERS

For those that have not experienced it yet, this may come as a shock when it occurs, but your characters are living people. Not literally, but, if you are writing a lot and getting into a story, you might think of them as separate entities.

A way this might occur is you suddenly refer to characters as themselves. You think, "Oh, Bob is going to hate when this happens." If you talk about a character as if they were a friend you know well, then you've started the path of making a new person.

Congratulations. Now good luck shutting them up in your head.

This is the most important aspect of creating a character. All else, all the methods and the talk and the lists and the outlines are in service of making this happen. This feeling of them becoming living agents. The absolute sureness, despite one's higher reasoning, that they are out in the world, or other worlds, doing something, and that you could feasibly run into them one day.

If you find a way to do this for yourself, all other methods of developing characters are pointless. You've found the goldmine. You've found the holy grail of storytelling and the guide that will get you through the toughest of your story problems.

Because, if you have an alive character that thinks and acts, then you simply create the initial scene, the initial danger, and other needed aspects of your premise, and then listen to what your character wants to do. They will tell you what happens next—the story will bend to their will, and you get to simply sit back and dictate their thoughts, feelings, and choices.

Sure, you may need to figure out what happens in the wider world, or stuff that the main character can't know—but the main bulk is half-done.

Writing like this can be thrilling, ecstatic, and magical.

Though, before I get you too excited, I do have to warn this won't always happen. You may write entire books without feeling this presence of a character's spirit. It can take a long time to find how you need to outline or envision a character to get them to sprint to life and move as not a puppet.

It's okay. Good books are written without this happening. Writing is strange like that. Technique and practice can get you through without inspiration. And good storytelling can get people to read and enjoy, even if you are not yet channeling the creative force that is propelling characters into "real people."

Once you find it happens—and I promise it will occasionally happen if you write enough—then note what you did and remember that you can make people come to life with the right steps.

Oh, and yes, them not shutting up until you finish writing their story is to be expected.

Have fun.

Assignment 3:

Creating characters is often a deeply personal process. Same with villains. There's no right way to do it. However, for the sake of being able to do it easier, I have steps for you that might spark ideas. I have some drills that will loosen blocks that might have been there before.

So, let's start rapidly making characters, shall we?

Step A:

1. Pick a genre. Need not be one you plan to write. It should be one you have at least read or watched enough to know some clichés.
2. Okay, now, come up with a fairly stock character. Like a loner cowboy for a western or an outcast teenager for a young adult urban fantasy.
3. Think up a villain the same way. Maybe think about some media you've seen and go over the villains or antagonists that challenged the main character.
4. Write down—in as little words as possible—what makes this villain and hero perfect for each other. Put this down on a piece of paper or typed in a document.

5. Repeat this process, as quickly as you can, ten times. You should start seeing some interesting patterns.

Step B:

1. Go through the villain type chapter and pick four qualities. Yes, you can have villains that do not fall so hard on either side of the categorization, but, for this exercise, we will be extreme. So, pick. As a reminder, the sections are:

   - Justified to Selfish
   - Moralistic to Immoral
   - Personal to Monolithic
   - Comedic to Dour

   You might have a villain who is a Justified-Immoral-Monolithic-Dour. Additionally, you should add one or *more* of these qualifications:

   - More Powerful
   - Smarter
   - More Experienced
   - Looser Morals
   - Access to More Resources
   - Access to More Allies/Henchmen
   - Knows More About Things

This is to determine how they are a threat to your hero. This can cover many genres and types of villains. For instance, a sports story might have a villain with better equipment, more time playing the sport, and is physically bigger than your hero. They then might be a selfish teammate who has it out for the hero, but only attacks through the medium of the sport (moralistic), was an old rival at an old school (personal), and is a rather serious player (dour).

Make a character, a villain, that is built within those lines.

2. Create a hero that connects to this villain. A hero that matches them and opposes them. You likely already came up with a lot of this as you were working on the villain.
3. Write down, even though you likely already know, how these two characters connect— how they might reflect each other.
4. Repeat this step three times. Quick as you can.

Step C:

1. Using the ideas in the first section of this book, generate a hero. They can be complex or fairly simple. Just a hero of a story. Need not be a story you intend to write.

2. Now, using the villain types, build a villain for them. You'll note this is the reverse of the step above. I want you to make a hero from a villain starting point and then make a villain from a hero starting point. Both are valid approaches, and I want you to get a feel for each.
3. Again, write down how they reflect each other. Do this three times as fast as you can manage.

Step D:

1. Look over the pairs you've listed. Now, for each one, I want you to create a theme their conflict represents. Is your conflict between the villain and hero representative of, say, the nature of power? If so, then great—it works for our purposes. Mark each theme. Come up with one at random if you can't think of something really fitting.
2. Now, in a story that has *that* theme, I want you to think of other people that might be engulfed by that concept. In our power example, you might consider politicians, superheroes, magic users, or even just richer people. Anyone who might directly represent or is engulfed by your theme. Make a list of them.
3. Do that for all the themes you came up with.

4. Give each extra character a name. Each engulfed person. Give them names, and what their job is, and what they look like in five words. Five words for the whole description. Like this: "chef, blue hair, depressed expression."
5. Once you're done with all of that, go back and read everything you wrote. Look for repeating patterns across all of them. Now, make one more villain and hero pair, and one more bunch of side characters. Throw some real mental muscle into this one. You don't have to write them into a book—but I would not be surprised if you feel the itch to do so.

That may seem like a lot—but it is teaching you to make characters fast. Or to identify how you might approach character writing. It's only one way to do it but making sure your entire cast is coherent within one or two themes will make for a tale that engages a reader and makes them think about your story's meaning or theme or message.

Now, your story need not have a theme or a message or anything of that sort—but I think you'll find you wrote one in. It's kind of hard not to do so.

Anyway, now the second part. The more structural part. I'll admit, this next bit was hard to write.

Though characters carry a story, we should talk about what makes them have a path to walk.

Read on to the next assignment.

THE WOE OF THE MIDDLE

When a new writer attempts a story and then abandons it, I'm sure it's always around the middle of the book where it happens. I don't have hard facts, nor enough examples, but it makes the most sense.

That's because the middle of the story is the hardest part of a book to write.

Think about why. Everyone likes the gimmicks of a story and the rush of a new world initially. It's the part that might excite a writer into writing. It's the part that's been sitting in their head for the longest time.

But, when they get to writing it, they find that there's so much book to get through. So much stuff to write to get to the big ending they have planned. It's a massive gulf—and a brutal desert they do not feel equipped to cross yet.

So how do we get through the middle, and what can we do to make it less miserable? Well, a few tricks make it easier for the writer. Never let these become crutches but do use them when you need guidance.

In no particular order:

- The Sliding Scale of Nasty People
- Jumping to Relevant Times
- Three Magic Items

- New Weird Places
- Different Character Hopscotch

There are a lot more of these options than what I've listed, but here's a breakdown of how to utilize each one. Remember that you can layer multiple of these on top of each other.

The Sliding Scale of Nasty People

You may have the main villain; you may have someone who the goal is to beat—but you can have people that need to be beaten first. This is especially common in fantasy shows, but it can work for just about any story that involves combat or a way to "win" or "beat" an opponent.

Your story is essentially a bunch of miniature stories, each one about a different enemy. The trick here then is to make sure that each villain is suitably different from the others. You can't just have the same storyline play out several times, each time with the hero winning.

Remember that you either have to have a reason each villain is gone (killing them is common, but might be out of the tone of the book) and that you can't rely on simply action scenes to carry an entire plot.

Jumping to Relevant Times

Sometimes, the plot of a book is annoying to write because there's so much travel or going to new places to do. You have an outline and a roadmap of cool and exciting and interesting things planned but have so much middle to crawl.

Well, you could just skip past those parts.

This can be very jarring and is better suited to shorter books or even short stories. But, instead of talking about that helicopter ride, that long walk through a war-torn area, or that spaceship flight, you can just end the chapter, tell the reader where you are now, and move to the next interesting part of the story.

Be sure to never cut out *all* small and quiet and slow moments. Those have a point in storytelling and can be pivotal to character development, but they need not happen all the time.

Three Magic Items

Doesn't have to be three, but it usually is. Your plot is then set into three mini-plots, each one around the getting of some magical so and so. Doesn't have to be magical though, can just be three relevant items or pieces of information or parts of a machine or whatever. They only have to be useful to solving the plot.

This shortens the time you have to go without something interesting happening. Often three guardians or challenges accompany the three items, which can act as little action or puzzle story moments. You can also fold the sliding scale of nasty people into this, and have one per item, and then one trap for each item, and one bit of lore per item, etc. Never allow this to be too repetitive, or formulaic, but the number three is very powerful in fiction. Use it for all its worth.

New Weird Places

Instead of a new person or item, you can also have your story go to new places in each chapter or each section. This allows for a good deal more fun world-building and also keeps the story feeling expansive and exploratory.

The only problem is this might run into very bad stereotyping if you are using real locations, or a breakdown of your world's logic if they are not real places.

Let me explain what I mean with both. The first one is simply that you are setting your story in a place that does exist, and has real people, and real culture, and, if you are not intimately familiar with it, you risk turning the whole place—and, by extension, its people—into a cartoonish, offensive, or simply inaccurately represented place. If you are representing it negatively, you might cause someone's opinion of a culture to lower—which is the exact opposite of your job as a writer.

You are a storyteller and thus have that power. Use it to increase empathy, not destroy it.

The second one is a matter for fictional worlds or countries. Assuming you aren't just using a stereotype as a template and thus doing the same mistake as above, you might break your world.

Countries exist next to each other, and if you have a place of no gravity right next to a town of rock people, you might create plot holes.

In worlds that aren't so focused on reality or realism, this may not matter. But remember, always, that aspects of your world or universe don't exist in a vacuum. Planets in different solar systems may not affect each other at all—but a town with magic next to a town with no magic needs some explaining.

Different Character Hopscotch

If your story has a larger cast or even just a smaller cast that does things independent from each other, you can leverage this for pacing.

The second that one character is traveling or incapacitated, swap over to another. You may need to keep track of a timeline, but you can use this as a way to pace a story.

Hell, you can even purposely switch during interesting times to another interesting time, thus forcing your reader to keep going to resolve both plots. This can be annoying if done wrong—but can make readers devour your book if done well.

Essentially, the benefit of not having a character who is always the point-of-view character is the ability to jump around and keep the pace tight. Just be sure to always heavily signal that you are switching and make sure to label what character we are inhabiting. Don't jump mid-chapter, unless you also clearly signal that is what you are doing. At the very least, a page-break or line symbol to indicate the switch should be present.

You can always use multiple of these and play with them in both numbers and presentation. The point is to make it so the plot never feels too slow or boring, both for you while writing, and later for the reader. If you have an issue with writing the middle of stories, then simply insert miniature versions of the beginning, middle, and end structure within a bigger story.

REPETITION AND MEMORY

A story that repeats itself too much is boring.

Stories that don't callback to or reference themselves are disjointed.

And it's the second one we need to address. Essentially, it is the simple plot fact that unless amnesia is at play here, your characters recall what just happened, and are affected by what happened.

What I mean is that if a character dies horribly, everyone around them will remember that fact. Characters can't just shrug off trauma and move on without ever mentioning it again.

If you have tonal shifts too rapid, without explanation or purpose, especially in stories with violent content, then you are signaling that your character is desensitized or flatly insane.

Like, yes, your story can't just crawl to a halt while the main character is unable or unwilling to continue the plot for hundreds of pages. But you have to write with the logic of the aftereffects of events, or your audience will be ejected from the plot.

Similarly, in a less morbid sense, if your main character witnesses something, or is told something, or is made privy to information, then you can't have them act in a way that would suggest they forgot that information.

If your character saw a password, and then you don't have something about it being too complicated to recall, then your main character now knows a password. If a character sees the specific rules for how to use a magic item, then doesn't use that information later when interacting with that magic item, then you've made an error.

Your audience will remember rules and outcomes and patterns, and you have to as well or they will consider it a plot hole or bad writing.

Essentially, always know what a character knows, and if different characters know different information that others don't… you need to keep track of that.

People are affected by the events that happen to them and will change based on such things. Either for good or for bad. You need to think about how the plot affects characters and not just how to make the plot go wherever you want it to.

CONSEQUENCES

Major story events must have consequences. Let me say that louder for the ones in the back: stories must have consequences, or the events of it do not matter.

But I mean this more than just the broad cause to effect that is most plots; I mean in the micro and the macro view.

You are, for the story world, a god who can make tiny and large alterations to the cosmos. You must have a steady hand, less the cascading implications ruin something. And, yes, you also determine the effects of that cascade, but you cannot hold back that cascade and expect anyone to care about what you do next.

If your story is set in the real world and something massive and supernatural just happened, like the sudden discovery of a giant evil sloth, or the sudden confirmation of magic existing, then you have to consider what that would do to our world, to our society, to our culture.

It's not going to be something light or able to be shrugged off.

That's macro-scale though, and if your character doesn't much interact with the world outside the plot, then you can just imply—but you still have to account for the micro. If a character hurts his hand, and then uses that hand to do complex motions, and does not have a healing power excuse, then you're violating your own rules.

If a character does something shitty, then the plot needs to treat them as someone who did something shitty. If a character suddenly becomes very powerful, either politically, magically, whatever, then you have to account for how they deal with that, and how everyone around them might feel about it.

My point is respecting the logic of your own story, and paying attention to the actual, real cause and effect of anything and everything you put into a story world.

Because the more you treat your world as a world with logic, the more your audience will do the same.

A QUICK NOTE ABOUT PLOT TWISTS

I am putting the rules about plot twists here because you need to think about them more in the middle. They often are a part of plotting a beginning, but the real meat is here.

This is because a twist needs to have a preamble. A strong mind-bending twist is true the entire time of the story, informs the entire flow of the story, and impacts the story heavily.

This means that whatever the twist is must be baked into the structure of the plot. The trick of a plot twist that will move your audience is that it is guessable—but that you've done all you can so they cannot guess it.

You do not lie. You do not exactly *hide* something…you simply withhold as little information as possible so an entire aspect of a plot is not obvious. Then it hits like a truck once it is known.

The best way to do this is to drop things into the plot, the dialog, the world-building, that seem wrong or suspicious or unexplained and then not answer them or even call attention to them.

It's a real cliché twist now for the main character to secretly not be human and not be on earth, but, if you must do this, and for the sake of an example, you might withhold information such as...

- That the sky color described in one scene in a way that feels like a metaphor is the real sky color.
- That the futuristic technology is not earth technology. You can make them think it's just a future-set story.
- Very mildly state anatomy facts wrong, so the clever-eyed will realize that's not how human organs work. This *can* lead to your audience simply thinking you did not do enough research—but it can be used this way.
- Something off about how many months, years, or seasons there are.

And a hundred other tricks like this.

The risk is that you do need to make it possible to guess. If it's not, then you're likely cheating at the rules of storytelling. Also, some readers *enjoy* figuring it out without help. Let them have that chance.

Twists are so beloved and desired by writers because they are masterpieces when done correctly. They can make stories iconic and amazing to revisit. But this can only happen if you do the careful work of planting the clues and still obeying the logic of the plot.

Assignment 4:

This will be a fairly short assignment (in terms of instructions, not in terms of how long it might take to do), as your characters should inform most of this.

Also, fair warning, this assignment will require you to have done the other steps in the book.

1. Create a book premise, and a villain-hero pair, and work out a theme. Essentially, take all that you've done until now, or create a quick version of them anew. You're going to need them to effectively do the next steps.
2. With all of that in mind, we will go down a Plot Flow. I'm sure someone has made something similar and given it a better name, but the idea is simply a way to move along a plot's train of thought. Go down this chain and fill in the blanks:

Plot Flow:

1. Everything was normal until_____
2. And then_____
3. There was no way to go back to normal because_____
4. So, the main character decides to_____
5. The main character does that until_____
6. Pick one or both:

a. But then____ / However____ / Until____ / And then____
   b. Because of <u>(previous thing in the story)</u> the main character____
7. Repeat #6 As Many Times as Necessary or Desired.
8. So, then_____
9. And then_____
10. Finally, _____
11. Which means that_____

End of Plot Flow.

Now, my Plot Flow method is rather open-ended, and very simplistic, but the point is to show that a story is structured on events moving into other events. Cause and effect are the bread and butter of storytelling. Each action causes another, and each action often—but not always—makes the situation more dire or dangerous or exciting. A character chooses a path, and that choice causes something to happen, and then both that choice and all further choices compound until the whole story is handled and done, for good or for ill.

Most of the rest of the book is specifically for endings, so don't worry if you are not sure how to fill out the ending bits of the Plot Flow. Just run a few story ideas through it as far as you can manage, then go again. The Flow is short and simple for that reason. It's more demonstrative—but I won't be surprised if you use it for plotting books.

Now, once you feel like you have a handle on flow and structure, let's talk about how to bring a story home, shall we? Read until the next assignment.

THE GOAL OF AN ENDING

Story endings put a lot of weight on themselves. They are, in all seriousness, what brings a story home, what determines what people think of a tale, and how willing they might be to experience your work again.

Your ending matters a lot, and you must treat it with that respect.

A good ending is a culmination. The moment cements all that came before. It must result from what has happened, explain most if not all of what has occurred, and not betray the emotions of the reader.

Your twists must be sensible, your character deaths earned, and your victories earned even more.

If you set everything up well and planned enough, endings naturally work, and stories will end themselves.

This can be literal. You may suddenly find that your fingers don't want to move. Not a writing block, but a simple gut feeling that the words should not come anymore because the story is done.

A sequel may be needed, but this book is *done*.

So how do we end a book properly? Well, that's the goal of the rest of this nonfiction book.

I can tell you this right now: it will require some tough thought and active decisions. Your ending determines everything, but must also match everything else, and honestly should have been planned from the beginning of the book. That way it can ring true. That way it can feel correct.

But we're here now, and you maybe don't have a plan, so let's talk about some more common things to look out for—in the following articles.

JUSTIFIED VICTORIES AND EARNING IT

This aspect of storytelling is hard to swallow, often ignored even by the most high-profile stories, and important to make an audience feel satisfied.

And that is an earned victory.

This can come up all the time in a story, not just the ending, but it's imperative not to mess it up at the end especially. Your audience may forgive it at earlier points in the story, but they won't at the very end.

If your hero is in a battle, and some magic suddenly appears—never mentioned before—that lets him win, then you've goofed.

If your romantic lead suddenly changes their mind, without a reason, and falls in love with the other lead, then you've messed this up.

If you make a story that feels like the solution to the final issue was earned with no cleverness, no persistence, no introspection, or growth, then you are writing a fluff ball of a story with no real stakes.

It does not matter if it is a story of combat or gambling or even baking for a contest, there's got to be a sense that the hero could not have solved/won the way they did if they were the same person as they were at the beginning of the story.

Classic superhero stories usually have this be a slow unlocking of greater power or at least an unlocking of understanding how their power could be used to win the day—but that's not the only way to do it.

You could have an old lady character with a fear of crowds overcome that phobia to win a cookie baking contest and secure money to keep the house she shared with her late wife.

A simple blueprint of a lot of stories are:

There's a problem. It seems bad.

It's actually really bad.

I am not capable of handling it as I am.

I try to improve myself and maybe fail a few times.

I become able to handle it or I think I am able to handle it.

I handle it or I actually really could not handle it.

You could do well to just follow that structure because it will ensure you have this point—this strength of having earned the ending of a story.

Now, there is a way that some stories will approach this idea, and while I can see the merit, it depends on the story if it will fit the tone. A story victory can be earned by a character deserving it, not earning it.

As in, the audience has seen this character receive no end of hardship, and the character has, along the way, shown their strong moral fiber or simple "goodness." They then get their happy ending.

You can use this, but you often shouldn't.

Mostly, a character must battle—literally or not—for the thing(s) they want, putting in massive amounts of concentrated effort toward it, and then growing because of that choice and subsequent choices until they can overcome the things that prevent them from attaining their goals.

This, of all things, is perhaps the most important aspect of the physics of storytelling.

ABOUT HAPPY ENDINGS

Despite what I have said in previous sections, there is one big rule about commercial fiction. Your audience assumes a happy ending, and you will face a lot of backlash if you do not give them it.

The only genre this is not true in is horror and sometimes dystopia/apocalyptic fiction. In these, a bad ending—if allowing the story to be scarier or more satirical—is accomplishing the goals of the story, and thus can be forgiven.

However, for literally everything else, there's an expectation. Woe for those who go out of this one box.

And I need to clarify this: I, personally, do not mind reading negative endings. You may be similar in this aspect. I think if the ending of the story is justified, then fine, go ahead. I'm on board if it makes sense.

But I am in the minority. People want happy endings. Even those who read not only for escapism still want that assurance in their own life that things work out.

People usually read fiction for fun, and, for many people, a story that does not go well is not fun.

So, I have to warn you: if you want a negative ending, you will need a good reason. If you can't tell me the thematic and dramatic and interesting reason you want your story to end negatively for your character, then you should make it a happy ending.

This is also why I said endings must be earned by the characters in the section above. Because, though not as bad as a negative ending, audiences also hate seeing a character get a good ending without deserving it.

Let me take you through a strange example of this that might illuminate my point.

What if I told you that someone won a raffle, but they won because they were so rich they could afford to buy thousands of tickets? That they then bought a fancy car—and they already owned ten—with that money?

That's a terrible story, and you might even be actively angered at the injustice of it. The character did nothing special and did not earn the right to something good happening to them.

Okay. Now, let's say a character desperately needs money to not lose their house. They will be evicted next week. They embark to win some major sports tournament and practice hard. Then they lose and lose their house.

Again, not satisfying. Does that make you care to reread or recommend that story?

No? Okay, now, what if we add that he finds a wallet with five thousand dollars in it and saves his house?

That's not great. Something about it just does not flow with expectations or structure.

Okay, so let's go through the big final example here that should bring it all home for this article.

Let's now say that an ill-fortuned boy needs money, or he will lose his house. He recently lost his job because his boss refused to let him go to a friend's performance in a stage play that he swore he would attend. But he went anyway. Then he got fired.

It's a week until he will be evicted.

And then he learns of a sports tournament for a sport he's always been interested in that has a massive financial reward.

He goes for it, and practices so much and for so long. He pushes himself so hard that he finds his lungs aren't working like they should anymore and can only do strenuous activities for short periods.

For a day, he even thinks it's all over and he will lose his house. He even yells at his friend who's been helping him out this whole time.

But, at the last moment, he works out a way to overcome his new limitations, makes up with his friend, and, just for the heck of it, also asks out a girl he likes and she says yes, but the date is going to be after the game.

Then he goes, and it's close, down to the wire, but he wins.

He wins and not only can he keep his house, but has a real chance at his dream girl, and maybe even has a future in the sport, even if only helping teach new players. He even has grown a stronger friendship with his friend and knows that he can overcome hardships no matter what the world throws at him.

Now that's an ending, yeah? Plenty of drama getting there, plenty of chances for things to go wrong. But, in the end, a happy, life-affirming take on the human spirit and perseverance against the odds.

Now, that may feel schmaltzy to you—but all I said was that the ending needed to be happy. You can make the rest of the story brutal or bleak or even nihilistic, so long as you bring things home, so long as it makes it feel like the journey was worth it.

You can be sadistic with a story if you end it happily.

It's a rule that may annoy, but everyone does love a happy ending.

THE GREAT FALSEHOOD, TRICK, AND MISDIRECTION OF FICTION

Fiction is built on two big lies, and each takes an active effort on your part to make people believe it. One is intrinsic, and the other is expected, even if no one often speaks about it directly.

The first lie of fiction is that any of it is real. That it is not just mental spinning wheels and plates given form and direction by paper or the screen. That's the magic of fiction, but it's also a lie we all agree to just believe.

The second lie is much stronger, and it's up to you a lot more to convince the reader of it.

And that is the lie of unpredictability, of chaos, of chances of failure.

Look, barring very obvious examples, most stories will end happily, with the main character succeeding, with humanity winning, with the world not blowing up into pieces. Barring some examples, stories are very predictable in their core structure.

People have read enough stories to know that the hero wins his lady love, slays the dragon, and probably even gets some gold along the way.

And yet, when the main character is avoiding the dragon's snapping jaw, we still, somehow, if the story is told well, worry he might get eaten. We worry that the main character will not win this fight against the villain.

We buy into the drama, no matter how well we know it cannot end poorly.

Good stories, good story climaxes, trick us somehow into believing we do not know how it will go. We tense in our seats; we chew our fingernails, despite it all being a foregone conclusion.

This is the main power of the negative ending, actually, but also why you should not use it.

Because the *existence* of bad endings in stories *threatens*. Your story, the one being read, could be in the small minority and have a negative ending.

That doesn't mean most readers will want it to be, just that the possibility is enough to keep them on edge.

But you must keep them even further on edge. The lie must be buried in the unpredictability of moments, of specifics, and in-between outcomes. Bad outcomes that delay good endings are great and do keep some degree of chaos in the story. Yeah, your reader can just see how many pages are left in the book to figure out how badly you still may make things go, but those people will guess it all anyway. There's no point in trying to trick people who derive enjoyment from figuring out the plot before it occurs—let them do their own thing and have their fun.

For everyone else, those in it for a good feeling and the culmination of a story, make it so they cannot guess the moments that get to the ending, even if the ending is assuredly a good and happy one.

TYING UP THE SHOES OF A PLOT

Your plot should not introduce anything major you do not plan to handle by the end of the story unless you want to handle it in a sequel.

If a magical crowbar is discovered that can open doors, and that is the only magical item in the story, in a world with no magic, and it is never explained why it is there, then you have not handled it. Unless not explaining is part of the joke, in which case you are playing with comedy.

And that's different, but also not. You still handled it the second a character goes "what the…" and then shrugs it off.

It's, for the audience at least, not dramatically energized anymore.

That's enough.

Sometimes.

This can also be applied to broad story ideas and structure.

The point is classic, and you've probably heard it before, but don't add in "you should never push this button" as a piece of dialog if that rule will not be broken or dramatically followed. Similarly, don't give a character a flaw or a magic a weakness and then not have it play any part in the story.

Everything big you set up should be utilized later, somehow. Audiences love when stuff comes back into play from before—especially in unexpected ways. In fact, the more you do this, if you do it well, the smarter your audience will perceive you and your story.

You can vastly elevate a tale just by this attention to details.

Assignment 5:

To teach you endings, I want you to look back at beginnings. To teach you endings, I want you to think through logic chains. To think through endings, I want you to be optimistically pragmatic.

These steps will be short and fast, and I want you to do them twice. Once by writing them down, and then once exclusively in your head.

You will get to have a story outline when writing a real book, but learning to think it without visuals will ingrain it harder, and make it so you can come up with endings at the drop of a hat if you ever find yourself in need of such a skill.

So, here we go:

1. Write an ending, then give it a beginning. Yes, really. Do it backward. Be as vague or as comically complex as you please. "The villain finds out he was being manipulated and kills the secret real enemy of the story," is an ending. I'll give you that as a starting one. Now come up with how a story like that might begin. Come up with three potential beginnings to that story, all different. All different genres.
2. Okay, cool, now, come up with two new endings, and then come up with three

beginnings—different genres—for each. You should have nine beginnings and three endings.
3. Good, let's go more granular with it. First, let me give you the starting point: "In my uncle's shed there is a large wood carving of a mermaid wearing a sweater, it's tail covered in stickers that his old coworkers placed there each time they visited." Okay, now, you will come up with two things here. You will write down an explanation for the history of that object, and how it came to be in that shed. Then, you will come up with how, a few chapters later from when it was mentioned, it might play a part in a story.
4. For that mermaid prompt, come up with a reason that does not include magic if you included magic in your choice. If you didn't, come up with one that does heavily involve magic.
5. Here's five more prompts. Do the same for them. Any genre you want.
    a. "The ice was thin that year. The lake had not frozen nearly as bad as it had the last few. They'd warned us not to go on it. They didn't need to warn us, no one would after what happened."
    b. "I entered her room, and it was filled, floor to ceiling, with stuffed bears. Each of them had a little name tag and wore the same uniform that I always saw her

      in, that flowing green shirt with the pattern of honeycombs on it."

c. "What Henry discovered then was that the wax would not melt. Could not melt. Even a flamethrower produced not but a rush and roar as it impotently sprayed heat."

d. "The god leaned down and said to me 'this sound can only be heard by the darkest of our kind. The gods and demons we do not speak about or wish for humanity to ever meet. Use the horn wisely, for all of them will hear—not just the one you wish to deafen.'"

e. "He never said anything about it, but there was always a folded piece of paper in his wallet. It looked like a dog had chewed on it and was stained with coffee. But ask or even imply its existence and he would dodge the question."

And that should get you going. Should get you thinking. And, hopefully, help you along.

But now we've come to the big one.

The big assignment.

Assignment 6 and Beyond:

Do you feel like you can tell a story with coherence, with a strong plot, with a satisfying ending?

Do you feel like you can do it the next time you sit down to write?

Well, let's test it, shall we?

1. Go back through this book and reread the assignments. All of them. You need not reread the articles, you just need to see all that I have asked of you and recall (or look at what you wrote down as you went along) what you did for each step.
2. Write a short story. It doesn't have to be over twenty pages. But should be long enough for you to explore the rules and precepts and strategies I have taught you. Begin by outlining the plot of this short story. Just something rough.
3. Going over my instructions, make a villain and a hero and a few side characters. Then, use the Plot Flow to further nail down how the story will progress. Get a strong sense of both the literal plot and the emotional flow of the story.

4. Write it. Once you have, leave it alone for a week. Then, reread the story. See if it seems different than anything you've written before.

Meanwhile, while you wait for that week, you've got more to do. You will always have more to do.

I assign you a large task. Call it an exploration. It is ongoing and is to be done anywhere and anytime you can.

Your task is to learn.

Your task is to observe.

Your task is to take in the world for the sake of stories.

Authors improve by reading fiction, and seeing movies, and researching, and studying technique, and style, and the history of writing.

But also, they learn by studying practically the entire breadth of human knowledge.

The freedom of the writer, to the point of almost being a cliché, is that we may ask almost any question and study any topic if it is for the sake of a story. Almost no one will ever question you.

Most writers I know have studied some wild stuff for the sake of knowing it.

Don't expose yourself to things that might deeply scar you, but your curiosity is almost as important as your imagination.

Your curiosity is the hunger pangs of that imagination.

Feed it and feed it well.

I want you to never rest on your laurels and assume you have a strong enough grasp of stories and writing. You are never done learning. Go get books on craft. Try out different ones from many authors.

There's always more.

There's so much more.

I tried to share here, with this book, some part of what I've learned in writing many novels. I hope my assignments have shown you new ways to write stories or strengthened your skill at certain aspects of storytelling.

That's the point of this series. To help make artists. To revitalize artists. To give them tools so they can succeed.

I hope I've done that for you.

As always, I will leave you with inspiration. Something I wrote from the bottom of my heart. Something to get across how important this artistic work we do is.

I hope you like it.

We are artists. We are creators and entertainers and dreamers. We are, no matter how society may treat it, an important part of culture.

Without us and the millions who have come before us, there is markedly less joy, less imagination, and less hope for the future.

People will fight, and hide, and die for art. They have throughout history. There's a reason that evil men try to burn books.

Art is more than art.

It is a powerful thing in the world, capable of the greatest change, and the most personal of inspirations.

People with no money will still go out to see movies.

Thus, we have a point here in our existence. And the job can always be done better.

By agreeing to be an artist, by learning to do it well, I am treating you as an agent of art, and, by being one, I feel you are responsible for something.

Your job is to be a point of light. To bring people together, or celebrate something beautiful, or smash down those that would threaten humanity. Art is a weapon, and a balm, and a meeting place of ideas.

Your job is to show humanity what it is because it may sometimes forget. Your job is to make a place that someone in their darkest times might find and feel calm for a while. Your job is to decry evil and show it can be defeated.

Your job is to excite someone. To make them smile. To get your audience to feel the cleansing rush of a good laugh, and the cathartic embrace of a good cry. Your job is to give those that need it assurance they are not alone in the world.

Your job is to give the world more beauty.

And believe me, even the art that only you see has added that to the universe.

To this end, you must learn about people. You must learn how others beyond yourself are. No matter how fantastical the world your story is in, you must present humans as human as you can.

You must practice so you might improve. You must learn from others and then decide for yourself through testing and observation what is workable for your own art.

You must find your soul. For each person that does will be a force for good.

Because I believe that when we find ourselves, when we discover what we are beyond the body, beyond the simple day-to-day existence, we are all good.

I believe that at the core of humanity is something worth saving.

You must seek it. You must help others find it.

Artists that have not yet made it to where you are must be assisted.

More artists must be made. More artists make for a better world.

As you get better, you must take others up with you. Selfishness has no place in the world of art.

But you, the person, do have a place in this world.

I declare you an artist.

Though you always were.

ACKNOWLEDGMENTS

You may have noticed that I don't usually put Acknowledgments in the back of *Actually Author* books. I don't have a really good reason as to why. It's just not been something I've thought to do. But this book is different, it's the third one. It completes a little mini-cycle that, even if I write many more books in the series, is complete in its creation. One book for new writers to get them writing, one to get them writing very fast, and then one to get them writing better books as they do.

And it feels like a good time to thank everyone who bought the books in the series so far. I never imagined it would become as popular as it already is. I've been a writer and an author for a long time, but to think so many of you have read my non-fiction… it's a little mind-boggling. It makes me actually giddy to consider.

I sincerely hope that what I've written gave you several tools to achieve your dreams as a writer. I want more people to be artists, and these books are how I'm currently working towards that goal.

And, since this *is* Acknowledgements, there are people in my life that made this book possible that I want to thank.

The first is my girlfriend, Aurora. I cannot begin to describe how lucky I am to have her. I hope she knows just how proud of her I am.

The next is my mother and my father, whose aid has been… well, how is a person supposed to ever express how much their parents do and have done for them? I thank them from the bottom of my heart.

The next is my grandfather, who I'm betting never expected the gift he gave me would spawn a whole series. His help is the reason there's a second book, or indeed this third one.

And then there's my writing group and my other author friends. I can see each of us growing, and it makes me happy and inspired in ways that I cannot easily express.

I'm fortunate enough to have a lot of amazing, wonderful, incredible people around me. I may not always let them know, but I see the things they are accomplishing—the hard work they are doing. I'm not an open person, but through these words, I can at least touch on my thoughts. I can at least put them somewhere they might find.

I can put out into the universe how impressed I am by my friends. I can talk about how even more competent I've seen my sister grow to become. I can let them know in some small measure how much they all mean to me.

There's really so much more to say, some of which I do not yet have words to express. I never can thank enough people in these things.

I just... this series has been something special. I hope it continues to be. I'm certainly excited to see where it goes.

ABOUT THE AUTHOR

From a young age, Brandon Scott realized he was tired of stories where all the characters survived, and the good guys always won. And, after flirting off and on with the idea of writing for a few years, he got his first disturbed shudder out of a reader. Since then, Brandon Scott has been chasing that same shudder, penning dark speculative fiction stories of various lengths—some of which even he can't think about for too long without his stomach tightening.

When Brandon Scott is not writing, sleeping, cooking, or just busy with life stuff (a rare thing indeed) he enjoys anime, books, movies, television, dumb online videos, and really anything you might call "nerdy" or "geeky." He lives in Florida and somehow still manages to feel cold.

Printed in Great Britain
by Amazon

15436103R00079